GET STONED AND READ THIS BOOK

by Gordon G. Gourd

A GORDON G. GOURD PUBLICATION

Gordon G. Gourd, Inc.
PO Box 833
North Kingstown, RI 02852
www.get-stoned.com

Printed in Hong Kong

For info contact Gordon G. Gourd, Inc. through www.get-stoned.com.

ISBN 0-9673537-0-X

Third Printing

Special thanks to all that deserve it. You know who you are.

Dear Reader:

We smoke pot.

It's not quite as taboo as it used to be, but it's still weird to admit
this to the general public. But we do.

This does not mean that we're activists. This is not a political manifesto.
This is not 'tune in, turn on, drop out'. We are not role models.

Say it with me. We are not role models.

But don't think that all we do is get stoned. Not true.

We're college graduates. We live with our girlfriends. We've actually
been employed in the work world for over five years. Each.

And we've worked hard. Answering phones, dealing with clients,
dealing with politics.

Shitty stuff.

We've also been known to spark a j, binge drink, and occasionally
do hallucinogenic drugs. Fun stuff.

But we're not Hunter Thompson, either (ether?). He was the king.
Some of the shit he did scares us. We don't want to be Hunter Thompson.

We just want to be a couple of gourds.

We laugh a lot. We like to have fun. We like to take pictures. We like to
think about shit. We figured we'd share some of our stories and ideas with
the rest of the world. That's what this is. Simple.

So get stoned and read this book.

The only problem is: how do we explain it to our parents?

Anyway, hope you like it. Thanks for your time.

Sincerely,

Gordon G. Gourd

To Cheryl and Melissa.

For putting up with the binges
that made this possible.

Thanks for everything.

wake n bake

The Anatomy of a Drug Tray

Rolling papers

Lighters

Metal skewer
(Bat–Cleaner)

Resin spoon

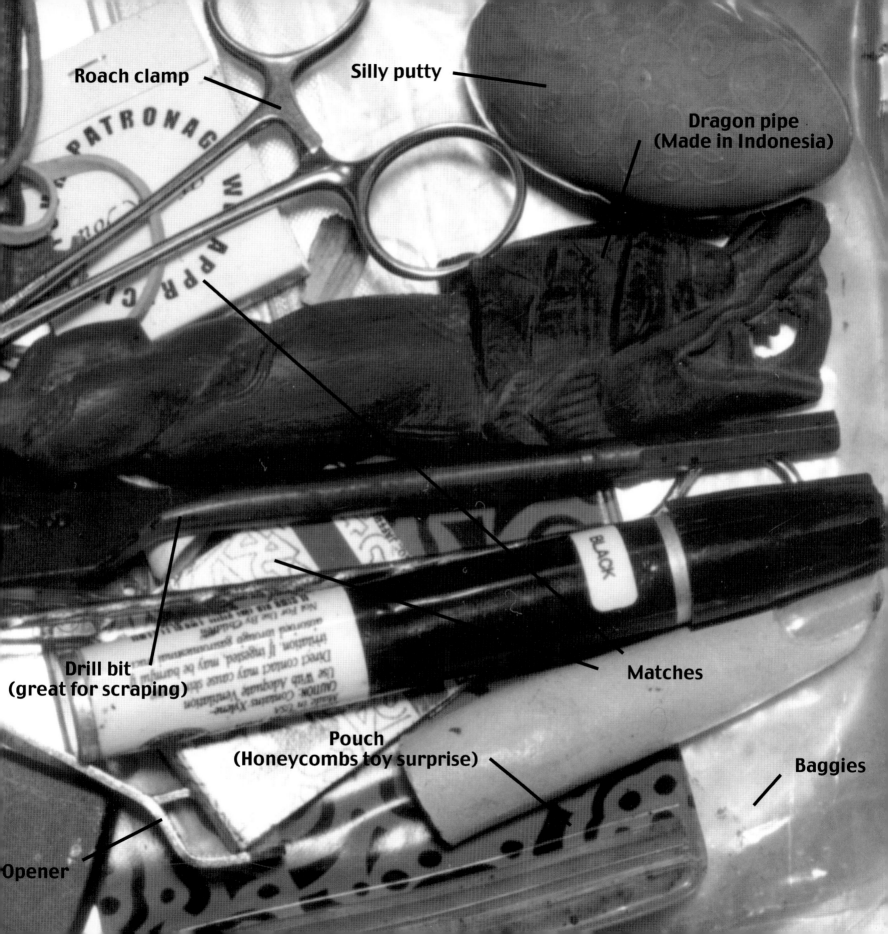

Roach clamp

Silly putty

Dragon pipe
(Made in Indonesia)

Drill bit
(great for scraping)

Matches

Pouch
(Honeycombs toy surprise)

Baggies

Opener

BLACK

not *too* shady

'Light, goddammit!'

'Oh, yeah....'

ode to my dugout

there once was a day when my bat would always be with me

wherever i went road whacks were a possibility.

i'd smoke in the street, i'd smoke in the car.

i'd smoke and i'd smoke, even whacks in the bar.

the boys, we were cool, doing whacks on the sly.

"pack it up again!" we'd say, "let's give it a try!"

we'd say "batter up!" when we got out on the street.

say "you wanna get high?" to the people we'd meet.

light it up, smoke it up, pack it some more!

bat hits and bat hits and bat hits, galore!

but now my poor bat is all beaten and chipped.

"it doesn't look like a cig now at all," someone quipped.

so i need a new bat to make smoking easy

and those brass ones, man, they look really cheesy.

so i'm buying a bat to get me back on track.

then wherever you see me, i'll say, "hey-- how 'bout a whack?"

One time I was playing caps at a party with three of my friends.
Dew-man and I sat on the floor about fifteen feet from Gary and Deke,
trying to throw bottle caps into the other team's beer.
This was the first time I had ever played caps, and I sucked.
I couldn't hit anything.

The game plodded along. They would make one. We would drink.
Dew-man would make one. They would drink. I just missed. And missed.
Finally I took a shot that hit off Gary's leg about two feet from the cup and I'd had it.
I was frustrated. I needed to relax.

I needed to use the Force.
I said to myself, 'All right, reach out and feel the cup.'
I took a deep breath.

Relax.

I broke into a big grin. Cheshire grin. I thought, 'I'm going to hit three in a row.'
I knew I was going to hit three in a row.
And not only was I going to hit three in a row,but after I hit the first one,
there would be some sort of a pause, some break in the flow, and I would say, 'Leave it'.
And then I would hit two more, and the fourth I wasn't sure.
But I was going to hit three in a row.

The rotation of the game was Dew-man, then Deke, then me, then Gary, back to Dew-man, and so forth.
Each rotation has 15-20 seconds before you go again.
All these thoughts happened in those 20 seconds after hitting Gary in the leg.

Still grinning, I took my shot. Splash. Gary and Deke looked at each other-- a pause. I said, 'Leave it.'
I hit the second one. I hit the third one.
The fourth one bounced off the rim and out.
Gary and Deke were shocked.

I looked at Dew and said, 'I knew that was going to happen.' He looked at me funny.
He said that was the most amazing thing he'd ever seen.
I said again that I knew I was going to do it. He looked at me funny again.
He didn't believe me.

But I knew I was going to hit three in a row.
And I was still grinning.

When really fucked up

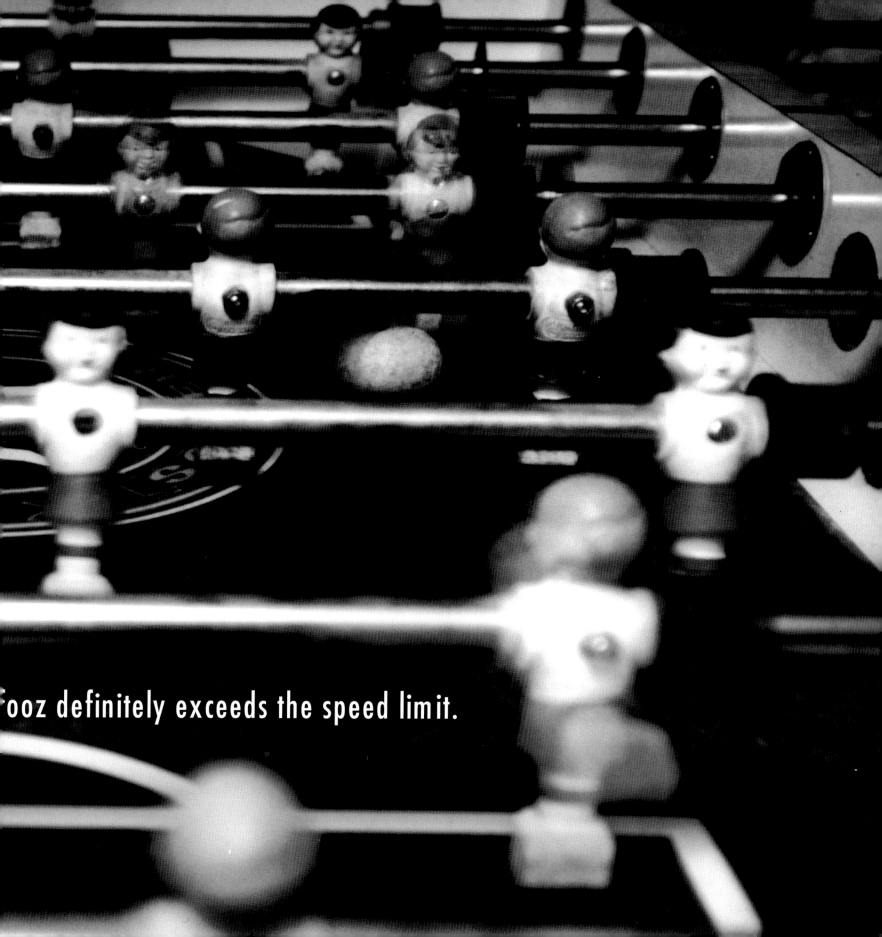

ooz definitely exceeds the speed limit.

I am not Tiger Woods

I love golf. But I suck.

I can't hit my driver.

I three putt. Often.

I change my ball every few holes

because I lost mine.

I play for my slice.

I get nervous on the first tee.

I hate eight-foot putts.

Sometimes I step in your line

(on accident).

I do bat hits on every par three.

And most par fives.

And on a couple of par fours,

depending on how my day is going.

Despite my failings, I still love golf.

I enjoy walking around for five hours

on a nice summer's day,

trying to hit that damn ball

into that damn cup

in anything under an eight.

I am not Tiger Woods.

I know that.

But sometimes,

every once

in a while,

I know

what

he

feels

like .

How to play Dahimi

Who: 3-5 players

What: deck of cards, no jokers

The object of the game is to get rid of all your cards (like asshole but better).

First hand:

Deal all the cards evenly, except the last four (last two if playing with five people). Leave these in the middle. Arrange your cards in numerical order three through ace, three being lowest. Twos, however, are higher than aces (this is weird, but you'll get used to it). A wild card (as yet to be determined) is higher than the two. So card heirarchy is wild, two, ace, king, queen, etc, three. Once you all are organized, everyone flip a leftover card (playing with five, wait a minute). The lowest card determines the wild— one number above the lowest card is the wild. The highest card goes first. The first one to play all their cards is the president. If a five is the lowest card, then sixes are wild (playing with five, flip now to determine the wild). Easy. The last one with cards left is the asshole. The asshole has to shuffle and deal the next hand. The wild changes every hand.

Now we play. Whoever drew the highest card goes first, and we go clockwise from there (if playing with five, whoever dealt goes first). He plays whatever he wants— a three. The next person has to play a four or better, then I play a five or better, etc. NO MATCHING. No three on a three, four on a four. You also don't have to play if you don't want to. Passing is a good strategic option. If a two is played, only a wild would beat it (wilds can be thrown at any time). When play gets to a point where everybody passes or a wild is thrown, whoever was the last to play gets to lead again, whatever they want. The first one to play all their cards is the president.

Wrinkle #1: playing pairs and triples. You may lead a pair. You may lead a pair. Even four of a kind. But you must play a pair on pair, trips on trips, etc. NO MATCHING. In these scenarios, a wild card is not a joker. If sixes are wild, you must play a pair of sixes. Or three sixes. Just remember, pair on a pair, trips on trips, etc.

Second and all subsequent hands:

Asshole shuffles and deals, leaving same number of cards in the middle. DO NOT PICK A WILD YET. When everything is sorted, the asshole gives his two best cards to the president, and the president returns his two worst. The vice-president exchanges one card with the vice-asshole. This is an honor system. Cheating will get you the asshole chair because someone will catch you.

Wrinkle #2: after cards are exchanged, the asshole flips a leftover card to determine the wild, same as before, one above the card flipped is wild (flip a five, six is wild). Keep flipping until the wild card is less than a ten (wilds shouldn't be face cards or up, but if that's all that's left pick the lowest).

Wrinkle #3: Here's where the asshole can get lucky— very often the president will give the asshole an eventual wild card. Begin play again, the asshole leads (another perk for the layman), with play continuing around the table taking the farthest route to the president, ie if the president is seated to the immediate left of the asshole, rotation goes to the right.

Wrinkle #4: bong hits can be called by anyone at anytime.

Play until you get bored. End play is just enough thinking to enjoy it, and not enough to get real frustrated (unless you keep losing). If this is confusing, give it a few hands before you quit. It's a lot of fun.

And you don't have to get up.

play ball cool papa bell three finger brown tinker to evers to chance mr october
teddy ballgame the yankee clipper the mick hammerin' hank ol satch I don't
believe what I just saw dem bums louisiana lightning yaz mark fidrych joe
charbonneau baseball tonight the babe charlie hustle goose gossage junior
buck o'neill the pride of the yankees holy cow it is high it is far it is gone
the iron horse cal let's play two cy young ty cobb murderer's row the gashouse gang
harvey's wallbangers ya gotta believe bill buckner bucky dent the scooter shoeless joe the
sayhey kid the brooklyn dodgers is this heaven? shadowball gammons daily dingers catfish
the big red machine we are family roberto clemente the facade the green monster the hefty
bag the mighty casey has struck out no it's iowa how bout that? the splitter the spitter the
splendid splinter the bronx bombers willie mickey and the duke miller huggins casey
stengel john mcgraw billy martin sparky tommy torre there's a drive gothimlooking the pennan
bash brothers the sultan of swat campy jack roosevelt robinson the giants win the pennant

the giants win the pennant big mac the kid rocket joe pepitone harmon killebrew paul molitor robin yount george
brett the ryan express roger maris gil hodges mel ott mel allen red barber the tribe cubs win! cubs win! the show bif
pocaroba... poca balla! three up three down bases juiced sacks full ducks on the pond joe medwick pee wee reese we
willie keeler maddux glavine smoltz neagle millwood there's no crying in baseball going back to the wall we are tied
moonlight graham the spaceman vic wertz ralph branca al downing
steve trachsel fernandomania mr rickey mr finley mr steinbrenner
mr cub joel youngblood willie mccovey gil mcdougald scott mcgregor
steve stone rock raines spahn and sain mickey cochrane bobby murcer
safe at first! buy me some peanuts and crackerjacks beah heah
backbackbackbackbackbackgone ripcity show em where you live
stop squeezin im blue frozen rope come on five-one give it a ride
keep your head up deep and I don't think it's playable goodbye
mr spalding he's not a playa he just crush alot six to four to three
if your scoring at home or if your alone i'm sorry mr costanza george
is dead the art of hitting uke uncle charlie turn two now batting
for pedro borbon... manny mota it ain't over til it's over where have
you gone joe dimaggio this kid really makes things happen out
there big hurt tony gwynn boggsie rotisserie the fall classic a cup a coffee
phenom we win watch out for in your ear roy hobbs home run derby al kaline tom tresh ralph kiner
pesky's pole nettles chambliss rice pops gibson marichal drysdale koufax richardson dewey brooks frank eck brock
schmidt bench perez tiant lefty reg-gie reg-gie munson straw doc nails the ivy grover cleveland alexander walter
johnson christy mathewson jimmy foxx hack wilson dizzy and daffy josh gibson oh doctor! barnstorming joe buck
harry caray don newcombe don larsen orlando cepeda the alou brothers moose skowron the san diego chicken the
phillie phanatic the wizard of oz jeter ordonez arod nomar nomo hideki irabu-ya! brushback knockdown strikeimou
throwimout whats the guys name on first base who the guy on first base elston howard honus wagner rogers
hornsby bob horner buddy biancalana don denkinger mo piazza caminiti bags biggio down the line foul hit and ru
run and hit forget about the deuce ricky give im the heater smoke gas darts peas go in hard hit behind the runner
monument park where triples go to die today I consider myself the luckiest man on the face of the earth GO YANKS

It's a bad fish... swallow you whole.
-- Quint

what do you see?

exotic or erotic?

love?

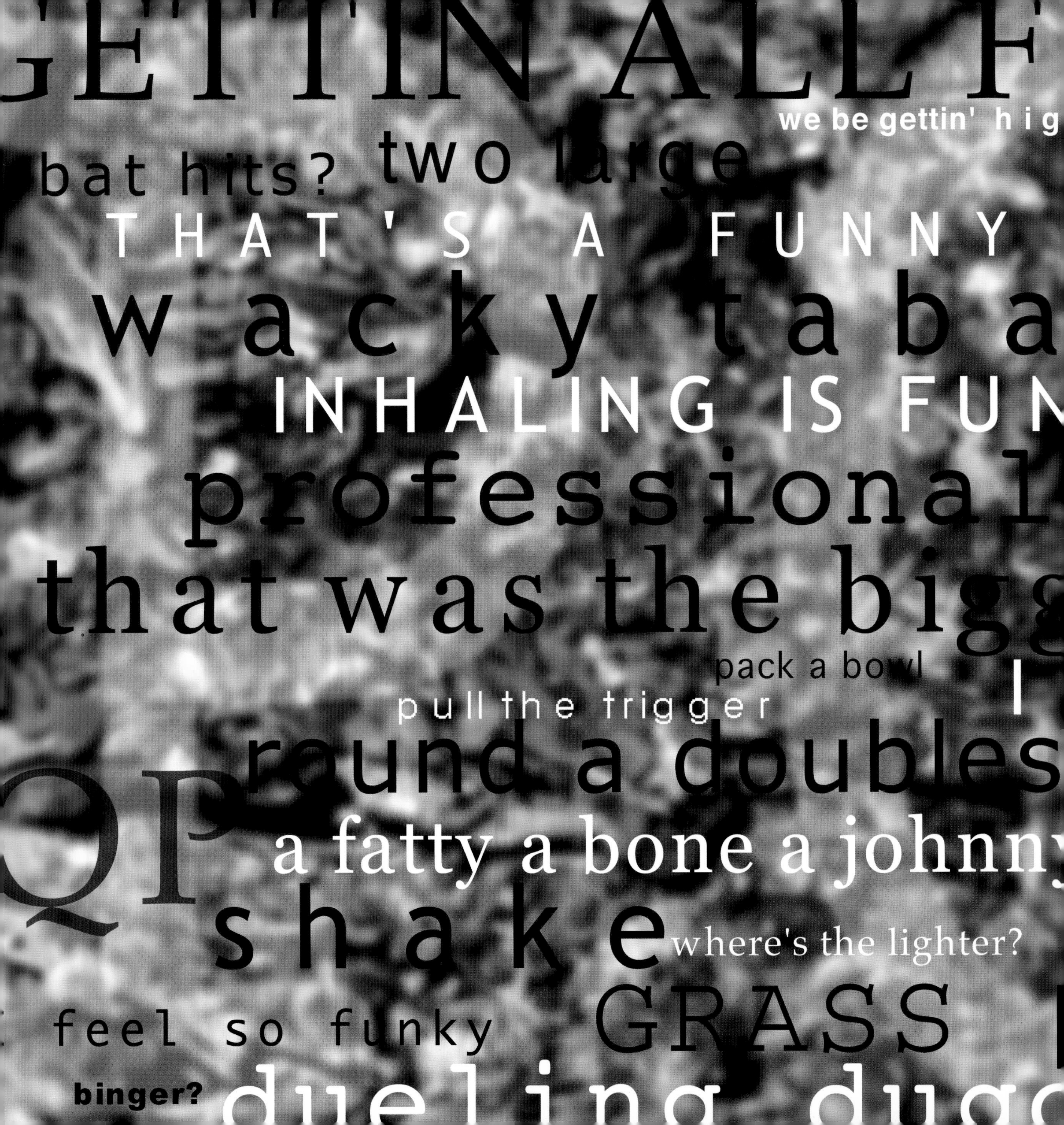

GETTIN ALL F

we be gettin' hig

bat hits? two large

THAT'S A FUNNY

wacky taba

INHALING IS FUN

professional

that was the bigg

pack a bowl

pull the trigger

round a doubles

QP

a fatty a bone a johnny

shake

where's the lighter?

feel so funky GRASS

binger? dueling dug

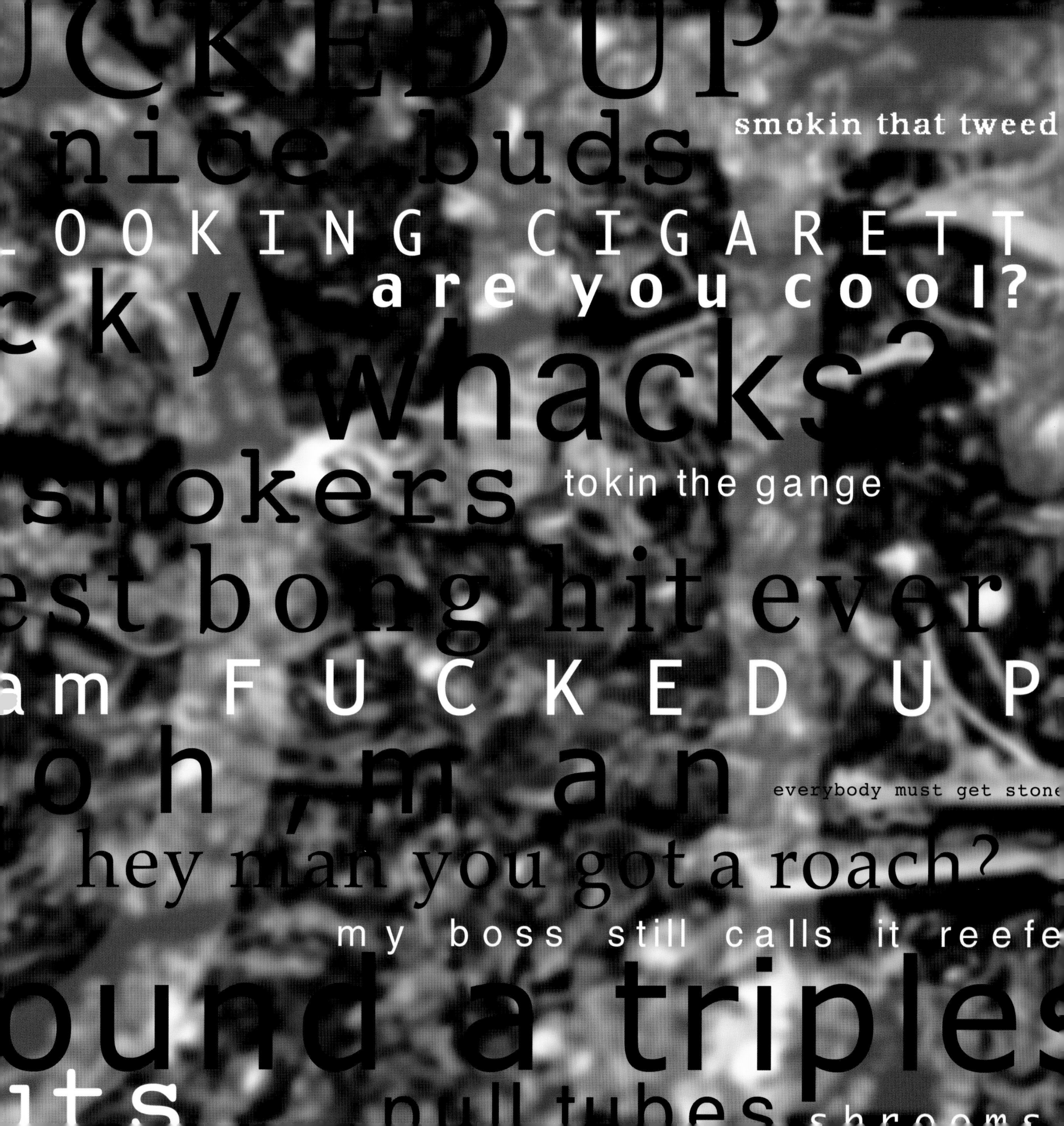

UCKED UP

nice buds

smokin that tweed

LOOKING CIGARETT

cky

are you cool?

whacks?

smokers

tokin the gange

est bong hit ever

am FUCKED UP

oh man

everybody must get stone

hey man you got a roach?

my boss still calls it reefe

ound a triples

ts pull tubes shrooms

This is Coco-Bean.

Lu-Lu.

boo.

whoa.

GO SOFTLY

Out in the woods. Four of us. Camping.
The fire was dying and
us all snuggled up in our sleeping bags
under the night sky.

As the fire receded, the dark crept closer.
No moon. Just stars. And dark.
Giggles and crickets and a breeze through the trees.
Just cold enough.

A meteor shower started soon after.
The sky was alive with streaks of light.
Whizzing across the night sky.

All of a sudden a brighter light shone down upon us.
From the heavens came this beautiful spectrum
an angel of colors to fight the dark.

Behold! The angel of colors shall conquer the night!
What ho! The dark shall fall to the victorious light!
Under the night sky.

But wait! The dark presses on.
The angel of colors screams as the blacks bleed back.
Little by little the colors fade.
Until blackness reigns again.
The black of the night sky.

Ah, the dawn.
Creeping up slowly,
sneaking up on the dark.
How glorious! The light!
Coming over the trees and the lake.
What a sight!

Holy shit. It's dawn.

I've been up all night.

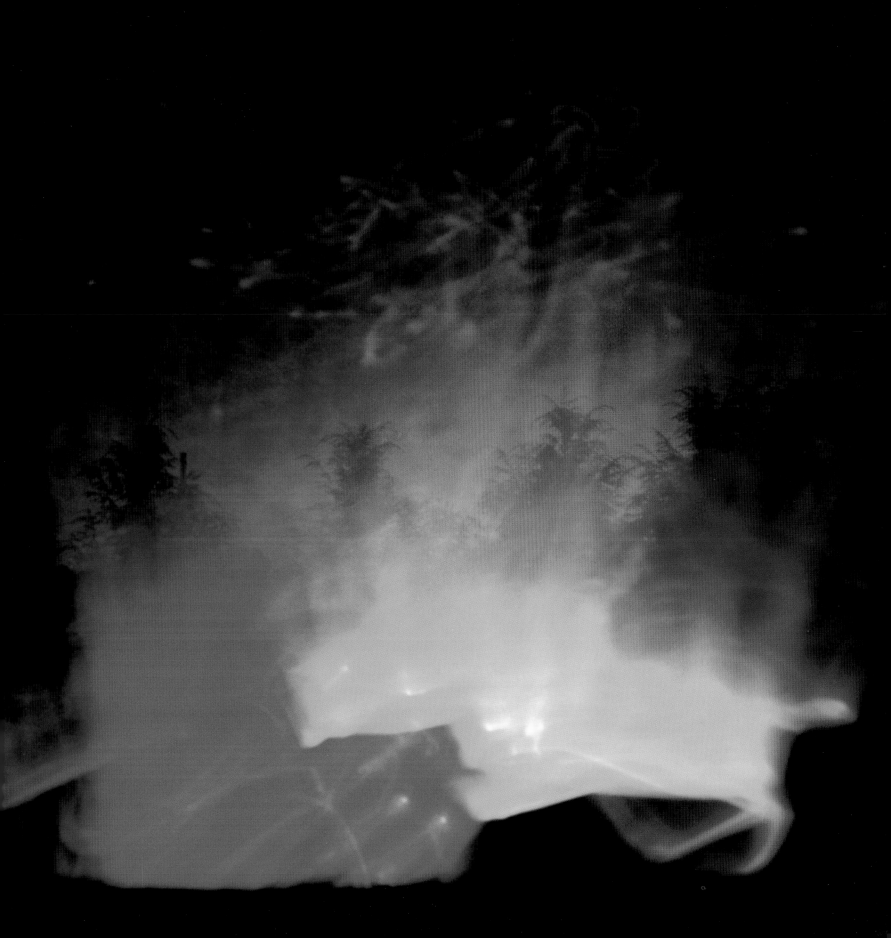

It was January last year, and my close group of drunkard friends and I were on our annual pilgrimage of excess in upstate New York. This was a special trip, however, because it was the first time that The Admiral had joined us. Our favorite place to booze up there is a bar in the middle of nowhere called The Heartbreak Hotel. Although it is a 'locals only' atmosphere, our excessive spending habits while in the midst of a serious binge make us well liked rather than merely tolerated. The bartender welcomed our boisterous arrival.

After about ten rounds of Killer Kool-Aid shot, The Admiral decided that it was time to step up the pace. He normally frowns at such behavior, but even he realized that it is necessity to completely lose one's mind on these trips. He jumped up on the bar and made a gesture to me.

I said to the bartender, 'This round is on The Admiral.'

The bartender looked at me and then The Admiral. Realizing that she was in the presence of royalty, she smiled at him and said, 'The rest of your drinks are on the house!'

VAGUE PLACE TO GET STONED   1448 Commonwealth Avenue, Boston

Football Saturday at the Phoenix. We've been fucked up for about four hours already and it's only two o'clock.
Halftime means halftime whacks-- time to take a walk (no whacks in the Phoenix). So we go outside,
walk around the block and get high. We've done this before. Two or three dugouts firing, multiple bat hits.
As we walk back down the block, we notice this park bench on the median overlooking Comm Ave.
"What the fuck is that doing there?" We walk over, take a look. A park bench that overlooks... nothing.
It serves no purpose. No bus stop. No cab stand. Absolutely nothing to look at.

"Wanna get high on the bench?"

And the Whack Bench was born.

ne

Ryan was my
your whole life.
into a room, see
And he knew that I knew wh

The next few moments are a bit

I spent the next two days between excessive binging and
post-meal entertainment. I'm sitting with the boys, and all

I look at him, and my mood immediately changes. I think to him
"Dude, you can't do that." "I'm going to-- 'Fitz, my friend j

About a year later, one
It was from BC's defeat of N

March 20, 1994.

The shirt read, "The mind, the body, the spirit, the soul".
Hedonism in Jamaica. We were so excited. Four of us,
on a plane, going to Jamaica, going to HEDONISM.

So we get there, we get on a bus to the resort and we start getting high.
All fucked up. We stumble off the bus, go to our rooms, drop our shit, and
hit the beach. Hedonism is one of those all-inclusive places, too, so we eat
and drink as much as we wanted, whenever we wanted. A glutton's paradise.

The trip pretty much goes that way until Wednesday. That afternoon, I
two pink phone messages in my room, one from my roommate back in Boston and one
from my mother, five minutes apart. There are no phones in the rooms there, so I
walk up to the main building to call home. All I can think of is my grandfather died.

rly in tears when I get the connection home. My father answers. "We've got some bad
He hands me to my mother (he has a tough time dealing with these things sometimes).
My mother gets on the phone. "What's going on mom?"

"Ryan died."

ar roommate at BC. That's a weird time-- being away from home, starting 'fresh' with
st friends. I describe our friendship as: we always had an inside joke on. I would walk
to somebody or pulling somebody's leg, and I'd know immediately what was going on.
on. He transferred after freshman year, but we stayed in touch. He was a good friend.

t have all the details, the service was today, he died on Sunday, his mom called, it's too late to fly to California.
I kinda just remember hanging up the phone and being back in my room crying to my friends.

otional wreck. Lots of crying. Just not real stable. At dinner that next night, I'm kinda sobbing, waiting for the
through the tears and my impaired vision, Ryan is there too, sitting in the empty chair across the table from me.

Ryan, I'm going to tell Fitzy that I'm too upset to go the bar myself, and I'm going to get him to get one for me."
uld you go get me a beer?" "Oh, man, that is so fucked up..." And I smiled. And he laughed, and he was gone.

My life has been different ever since.

rkers left my company, and left a mounted SI cover hanging in his cube. I still have it hanging in my bedroom.
a during March Madness. The date of the issue is March 28, 1994. The date of the game was March 20, 1994.

March 20, 1994. The day we left for Jamaica, the day Ryan died, the day my life changed.

I just found out about it four days late.

Sitting home alone on a Saturday.
This day is the one which
we look forward to;
so why am I completely bored,
feeling friendless?
The bourbon and ginger
call from the kitchen.
The dugout screams "Batter up!"
The stereo draws me
from across the room.
Countless selections,
songs for every state of mind.
The stereo is my companion,
fueling my emotions
anger, isolation, rejection, depression, distrust.
Don't answer the phone,
only intruders are there.
Time to kick back, have a smoke,
and turn up the volume.
This is temporary escape from
that ugly, cruel outside world.
Sorry people I can't hear you.
I'm in the middle of a
serious conversation with my friend,
the stereo.

The binge to end all binges was Gildea's bachelor party.

We got a little drunk on Friday night.

Woke up to bong hits at around 9am Saturday.

First beer was cracked at ten.

The festivities started at the Phoenix at noon.

The beer bus picked us up at one.

At the Phoenix South by 1:30.

Lunch. More beers.

To Newport by 3pm. Beers.

Shots started somewhere.

Back to the strip joints in Providence by 8pm.

Bat hits have been happening all day: on the bus, in the bars, on the street, etc.

Left Providence and arrived at M.A.'s by 12:30am.

Clancy and I are the last one's standing.

We go back to Beacon Hill,

drink red wine and do bong hits playing gin rummy

while watching Pulp Fiction and listening to Pearl Jam.

At 6am, we go to the corner store to get some eats.

Get home and make pasta.

Go to bed around 9:30am, Sunday.

Wake up at 11am, Sunday, and shroom.

All told, 60 beers between us, 30+ bong hits, 50+ bat hits, an eighth of shrooms,

and a pound of pasta.

This was the binge to end all binges.

fear

is learned
instinctual
ingrained

habit

rationalized irrationality
am i going to die?

who's there?
somethingjustmovedpastmyleg

fear

makes us hesitate
freeze

pounding

am i still breathing?
wake up

i'm right behind you

hate
anger

the dark side

borne of fear

death

mother?

stop scaring me
you must learn control
i feel... cold

open the door
go up the stairs
take a shower
look behind you

listen to the silence
listen to the screams

scare me
hate me
kill me
love me

fear me

Sometimes I just miss my friend.

...my ally is the Force and a powerful ally it is life creates it makes it grow its energy surrounds us and binds us luminous beings are we not this crude matter you must feel the Force around you here between you me the tree the rock everywhere *yes*

even between
the land
and the ship"

..Master Yoda

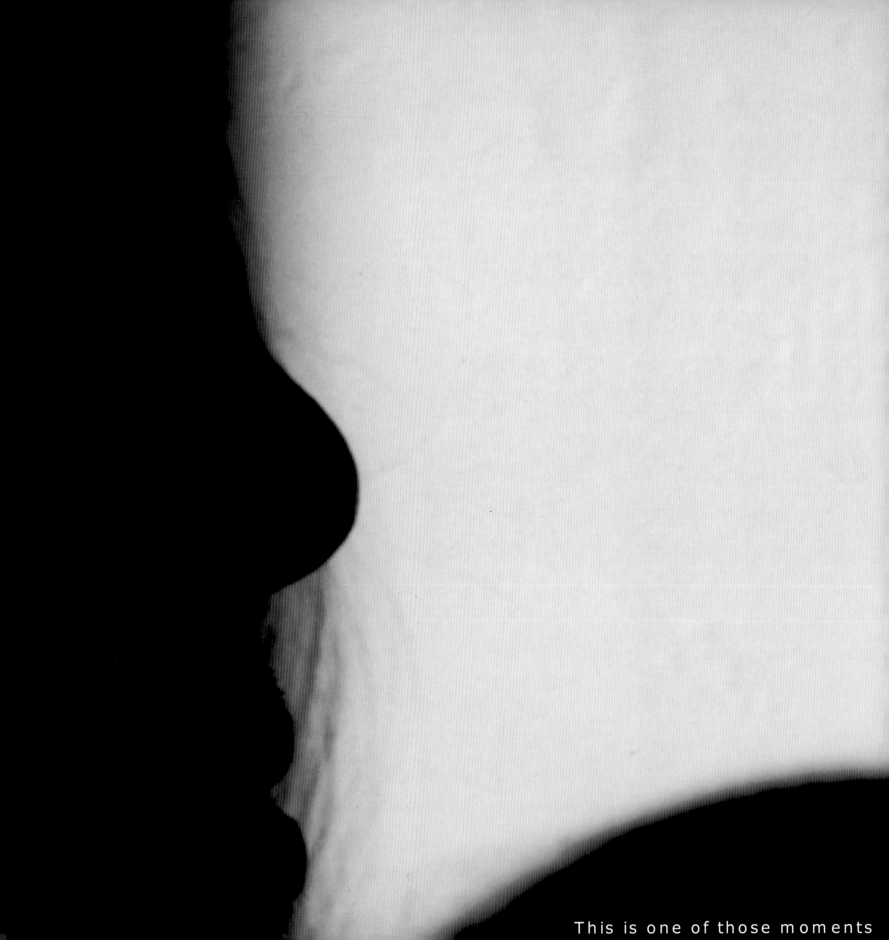

This is one of those moments

that mom will be so proud of.

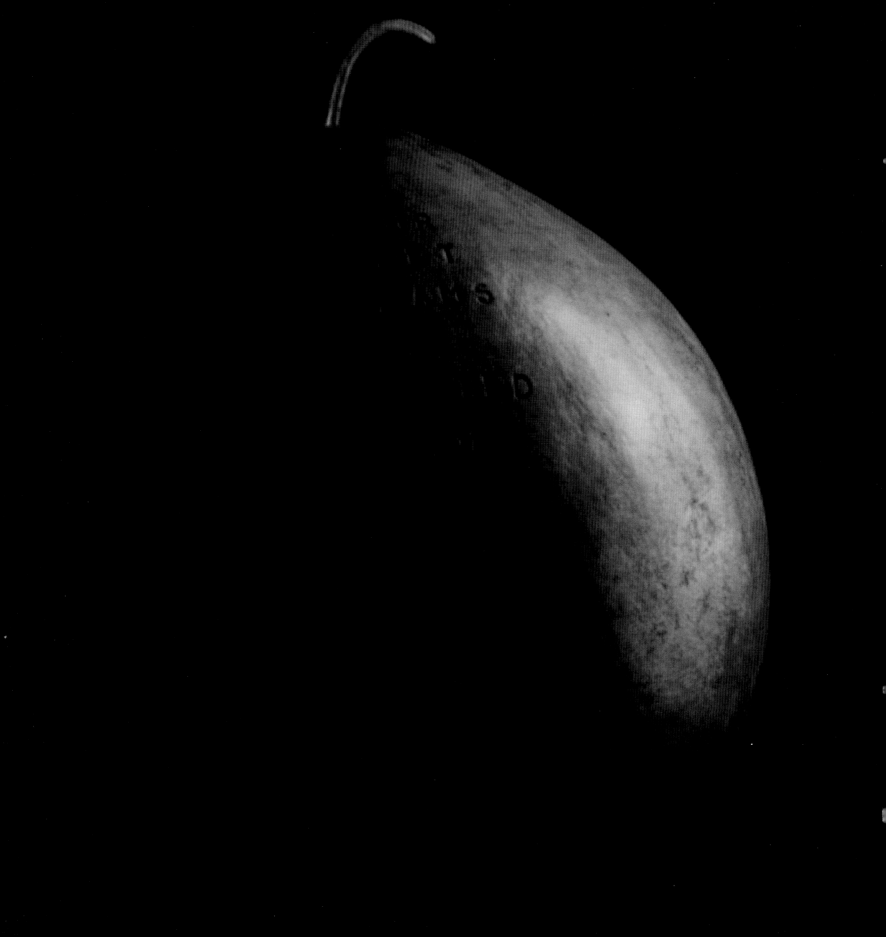

the origin of gordon g. gourd

it was the summer of 1995.

mr. clancy and i had been hanging out hardcore for over a year.

we'd get a little fucked up every now and again.

i picked up a little habit of telling him just how fucked up i was:

"clancy, i'm out of my gourd."

he'd reply, "no, you ARE a gourd."

soon after, he started calling me gordon,

and i made him in turn call me by my full, proper name,

gordon g. gourd

(the g stands for gordo).

now i call him at work, "tell him it's gordon."

he calls me, says the same thing.

great fun. gordon g. gourd.

we love it.

then his mother gives him this gourd the following christmas.

a gourd? for christmas?

"all your sweet dreams collected inside?"

weird.

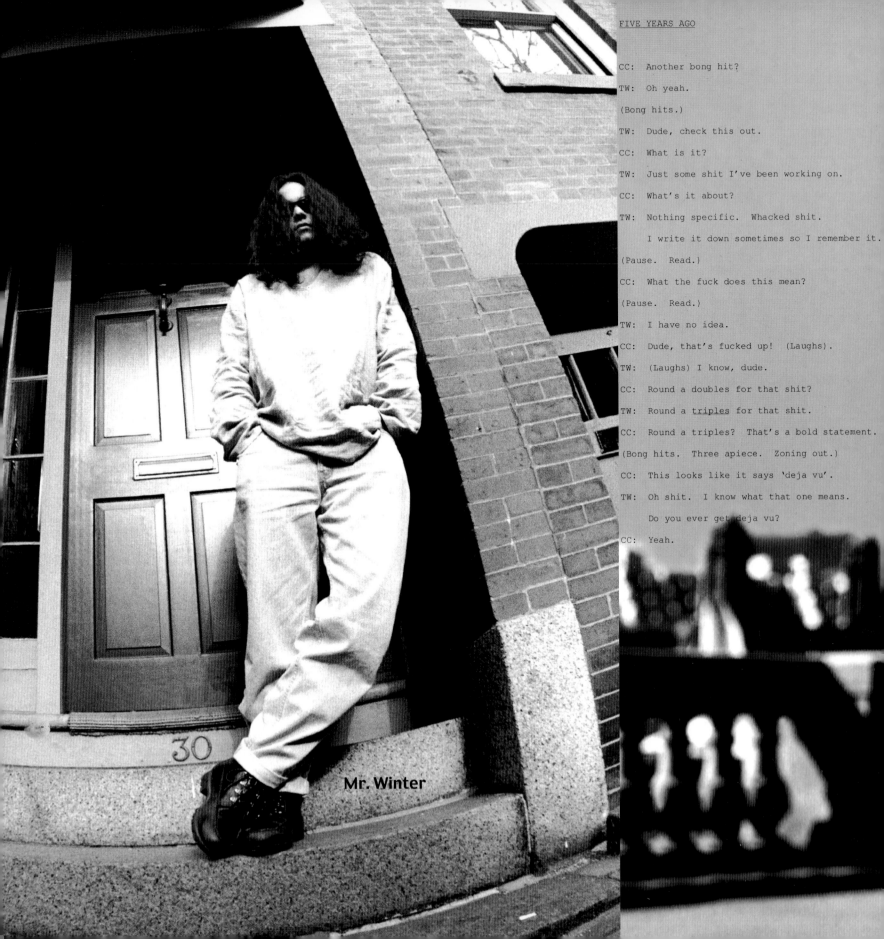

Mr. Winter

FIVE YEARS AGO

CC: Another bong hit?

TW: Oh yeah.

(Bong hits.)

TW: Dude, check this out.

CC: What is it?

TW: Just some shit I've been working on.

CC: What's it about?

TW: Nothing specific. Whacked shit.

        I write it down sometimes so I remember it.

(Pause. Read.)

CC: What the fuck does this mean?

(Pause. Read.)

TW: I have no idea.

CC: Dude, that's fucked up! (Laughs).

TW: (Laughs) I know, dude.

CC: Round a doubles for that shit?

TW: Round a _triples_ for that shit.

CC: Round a triples? That's a bold statement.

(Bong hits. Three apiece. Zoning out.)

CC: This looks like it says 'deja vu'.

TW: Oh shit. I know what that one means.

        Do you ever get deja vu?

CC: Yeah.

TW: Dude, I get crazy deja vu. Like, sometimes
    I remember dreaming about something and then
    it happens exactly like I dreamt it. I mean,
    I can remember thinking, "That was a weird thing
    to dream." And then it happens. It's fucked up.

CC: That is fucked up.

TW: Alright, ready for this? Let's say for argument's
    sake that I actually am remembering a dream when I
    have deja vu. That means that at the point when
    I dreamt it, I was seeing the future.

CC: What?

TW: Okay. I think when I have deja vu I'm
    remembering a dream. That's my definintion
    of deja vu-- that's what it feels like for me.
    So at the original point in time when I'm
    dreaming it, I was seeing the future, which
    is now my deja vu. You see what I'm saying?

CC: Yeah, dude. Totally. (Pause) Shit, man, I am fucked up.

TW: Me, too. (Pause) Shit.

(Pause. More zoning.)

CC: (Looking at the scribbles) Dude, I gotta show
    you some of my photographs.

Mr. Clancy

tomorrow

tired

going to sleep
ready to dream

of golf
pennants

s l e e p

flying?
soaring.

higher
and higher
and higher

so tired

up and up

into
the world of dreams

sleep

I could be a singer
(can't sing)
an accountant
(nightmares are dreams, too)

or a New York Yankee

fading
or a writer?
a teacher?

fast

a senator?

almost

an astronaut?

gone

a Jedi?

anything

remember

tomorrow

anything